Myron C. Fagan

The Illuminati and the Council on Foreign Relations

transcript of 1967 audio recording –
by Myron Fagan (1887–1972)

MYRON COUREVAL FAGAN
(1887–1972)

Myron Coureval Fagan was an American writer, producer and director for film and theatre and a red scare figure in the late 1940s and 1950s. Fagan was an ardent anti-communist.

The Illuminati and the Council on Foreign Relations
transcript of 1967 audio recording

Published by Omnia Veritas Ltd

www.omnia-veritas.com

[PART 1]

The question of how and why the United Nations is the crux of the great conspiracy to destroy the sovereignty of the United States and the enslavement of the American people within a UN one-world dictatorship is a complete and unknown mystery to the vast majority of the American people.

The reason for this unawareness of the frightening danger to our country and to the entire free world is simple. The masterminds behind this great conspiracy have absolute control of all of our mass communications media, especially television, the radio, the press, and Hollywood.

We all know that our State Department, the Pentagon, and the White House have brazenly proclaimed that they have the right and the power to manage the news, to tell us not the truth, but what they *want* us to believe.

They have seized that power on orders from their masters of the great conspiracy and the objective is to brainwash the people into accepting the phony peace bait to transform the United States into an enslaved unit of the United Nations' one-world government.

First of all, bear in mind that the so-called UN police action in Korea, fought by the United States in which 150,000 of our sons were murdered and maimed, was part of the plot, just as the undeclared by Congress war in Vietnam in which our sons are dying is part of the plot, just as the plot against Rhodesia and South Africa in which our sons will be dying is part of the UN plot.

However, the vitally important thing for all Americans, all you mothers of the boys who died at Korea and are now dying in Vietnam, to know is that our so-called leaders in Washington, who we elected to safeguard our nation and our constitution, are the betrayers and that behind them are a comparatively small group of men whose sole objective is to enslave the whole world of humanity in their satanic plot of one-world government.

Now in order to give you a very clear picture of this satanic plot, I will go back to its beginning, clear back in the middle of the 18th century and name the men who put that plot into action and then bring you down to the present – today's status of that plot. Now as a matter of further intelligence, a term used by the FBI, let me clarify the meaning of the expression 'he is a liberal.'

The enemy, meaning the one-world conspirators, have seized upon that word 'liberal' as a cover-up for their activities. It sounds so innocent and so humanitarian to be liberal. Well, make sure that the person who calls himself a liberal or is described as a liberal is not in truth a 'red'.

Now then, this satanic plot was launched back in the 1760's when it first came into existence under the name of the Illuminati. This Illuminati was organized by one Adam Weishaupt, born a Jew, who was converted to Catholicism and became a Catholic priest, and then, at the behest of the then newly organized House of Rothschild, defected and organized the Illuminati.

Naturally, the Rothschilds financed that operation, and every war since then, beginning with the French Revolution, has been promoted by the Illuminati operating under various names and guises. I say under various names and guises because after the Illuminati was exposed and became too notorious, Weishaupt and his co-conspirators began to operate under various other names. In the

United States, immediately after World War I, they set up what they called the Council on Foreign Relations, commonly referred to as the CFR, and this CFR is actually the Illuminati in the United States. And its hierarchy, the masterminds in control of the CFR, to a very great extent, are descendants of the original Illuminati conspirators. But, to conceal that fact, most of them changed their original family names to American sounding names. For example, the true name of the Dillons, Clarence and Douglas Dillon (once Secretary of the US Treasury Department), is Laposky. I'll come back to all this later.

There is a similar establishment of the Illuminati in England operating under the name of the British Institute of International Affairs [The Royal Institute of International Affairs]. There are similar secret Illuminati organizations in France, Germany, and other nations operating under different names, and all these organizations, including the CFR, continuously set up numerous subsidiaries or front organizations that are infiltrated into every phase of the various nations' affairs. But at all times, the operations of these organizations were and are masterminded and controlled by the internationalist bankers, who in turn were and are controlled by the Rothschilds.

The details of how they accomplished the setting up of the CFR in the United States as also in the other nations, are far too voluminous to describe in this dissertation. But you can find it complete in news bulletin #122 entitled *"UN is Spawn of the Illuminati"*, and news bulletin #123 entitled *"CFR Completely Unmasked as Illuminati"*. Both are published by the Cinema Educational Guild, PO Box 46205, Hollywood California. You can get them for 50 cents per copy by writing to that address.

Those news bulletins reveal the names of the original founders of the Illuminati and the Americanized names of their descendants in the present CFR.

Now I'll go back to the activities of the original Illuminati conspirators as revealed in news bulletin #122. One branch of the Rothschild family had financed Napoleon. Another branch of the Rothschilds, both branches the real masterminds of the Illuminati, financed Britain, Germany, and the other nations in the Napoleonic wars.

Immediately after the Napoleonic wars, the Illuminati assumed that all the nations were so destitute and so weary of wars that they'd be glad for any solution, so the Rothschild stooges set up what they called *the Congress in Vienna* and at that meeting they tried to create the first League of Nations, their first attempted one-world government, on the theory that all the crowned heads of European governments were so deeply in debt to them that they would willingly or unwillingly serve as their stooges.

But the Czar of Russia caught the stench of the plot and completely torpedoed it. The enraged Nathan Rothschild, then the head of the dynasty, vowed that some day he or his descendants would destroy the Czar and his entire family, and his descendants did accomplish that very threat in 1917.

At this point, bear in mind that the Illuminati was not set up to operate on a short-range basis. Normally a conspirator of any type enters into a conspiracy with the expectation of achieving his objective during his own lifetime. But that was not the case with the Illuminati. True, they *hoped* to accomplish their objective during their lifetime, but paraphrasing, 'the show must go on'. The Illuminati operates on the very long-range basis. Whether it will take scores of years or even centuries, they have dedicated their descendants to keep the pot boiling until, they hope, the conspiracy is achieved.

Now let's go back to the birth of the Illuminati. Adam Weishaupt was a Jesuit-trained professor of canon law, teaching in Ingolstadt University, when he defected from Christianity to embrace the luciferian conspiracy. It was in 1770 that the professional money lenders, the then recently organized House of Rothschild, retained him to revise and modernize the age-old Protocols of Zionism, which from the outset, was designed to give the Synagogue of Satan, so named by Jesus Christ, ultimate world domination so they could impose the luciferian ideology upon what would remain of the human race after the final social cataclysm by use of satanic despotism.

Weishaupt completed his task May 1, 1776. Now you know why May 1 is the great day with all communist nations to this very day. That was the day, May 1, 1776, that Weishaupt completed his plan and officially organized the Illuminati to put the plan into execution. That plan required the destruction of all existing governments and religions. That objective was to be reached by dividing the masses of people whom he, Weishaupt, termed 'goyim', or 'human cattle', into opposing camps in ever increasing numbers on political, social, economic, and other issues – the very conditions we have in our country today.

The opposing sides were then to be armed and incidents provided which would cause them to fight and weaken themselves and gradually destroy national governments and religious institutions. Again I say, the very conditions in the world today. And at this point let me stress a prime feature of the Illuminati plans. When and if their blueprint for world control, the *"Protocols of the Elders of Zion"*, is discovered and exposed, they would wipe all the Jews off the face of the earth in order to divert suspicions from themselves. If you think this is farfetched, bear in mind that they permitted Hitler, a liberal socialist himself, who was financed by corrupt Kennedys, the Warburgs, and the Rothschilds, to incinerate 600,000 Jews.

Now just why did the conspirators choose the word *'Illuminati'* for their satanic organization? Weishaupt himself said that the word is derived from Lucifer and means *"holders of the light."* Using the lie that his objective was to bring about a one-world government to enable those with mental ability to govern the world and prevent all wars in the future – in short, using the words 'peace on earth' as his bait – exactly as that same bait 'peace' was used by the 1945 conspirators to force the United Nations on us, Weishaupt financed, I repeat, by the Rothschilds, recruited some 2,000 paid followers. These included the most intelligent men in the field of arts and letters, education, the sciences, finance, and industry.

He then established Lodges of the Grand Orient, Masonic Lodges, to be their secret headquarters and I again repeat, that in all of this he was acting under orders from the House of Rothschild. The main features of the Weishaupt plan of operation required his Illuminati to do the following things to help them to accomplish their purpose:

1. Use monetary and sex bribery to obtain control of men already in high places in the various levels of all governments and other fields of endeavor. Once influential persons had fallen for the lies, deceits, and temptations of the Illuminati they were to be held in bondage by application of political and other forms of blackmail, threats of financial ruin, public exposure, and physical harm, even death to themselves and loved members of their families.

Do you realize how many present top officials in our present government in Washington are controlled in just that way by the CFR? Do you realize how many homosexuals in our State Department, the Pentagon, all federal agencies, even in the White House are controlled that way?

2. Illuminati and the faculties of colleges and universities were to cultivate students possessing exceptional mental ability belonging to well-bred families with international leanings and recommend them for special training in internationalism. Such training was to be provided by granting scholarships to those selected by the Illuminists. That gives you an idea what a 'Rhodes Scholarship' means. It means indoctrination into accepting the idea that only a one-world government can put an end to recurring wars and strife. That's how the United Nations was sold to the American people. One of the most notable Rhodes scholars we have in our country is Senator William J. Fulbright, sometimes referred to as 'half-bright'. His entire voting record spells Illuminati. All such scholars were to be first persuaded and then convinced that men of special talent and brains have the right to rule those less gifted on the ground that the masses don't know what is best for them physically, mentally, and spiritually.

In addition to the Rhodes and similar scholarships, today there are three special Illuminati schools located in Gordonstown in Scotland, Salem in Germany, and Anavryti in Greece. These three are known ones, but there are others that are kept undercover. Prince Philip, the husband of Britain's Queen Elizabeth, was educated at Gordonstown at the instigation of Lord Louis Mountbatten, his uncle, a Rothschild relative, who became Britain's Admiral of the Fleet after World War II ended.

3. All influential people trapped into coming under the control of the Illuminati, plus the students who had been specially educated and trained, were to be used as agents and placed behind the scenes of all governments as experts and specialists so they would advise the top executives to adopt policies which would, in the long run, serve the secret plans of the Illuminati one-world conspiracy and bring about the destruction of the governments and religions they were elected or appointed to serve.

Do you know how many such men operate in our government at this very time? Rusk, McNamara, Hubert Humphrey, Fulbright, Keekle, and go on and on and on.

4. Perhaps the most vital directive in Weishaupt's plan was to obtain absolute control of the press, at that time the only mass communications media, to distribute information to the public so that all news and information could be slanted so that the masses could be convinced that a one-world government is the only solution to our many and varied problems.

Now do you know who owns and controls our mass communications media? I'll tell you. Practically all the movie lots in Hollywood is owned by the Lehmans, Kuhn-Loeb & Company, Goldman– Sachs, and other internationalist bankers. All the national radio and TV channels in the nation are owned and controlled by those same internationalist bankers.

The same is true of every chain of metropolitan newspapers and magazines, also of the press wire services, such as Associated Press, United Press

International, etc. The supposed heads of all those media are merely the fronts for the internationalist bankers, who in turn compose the hierarchy of the CFR – today's Illuminati in America.

Now can you understand why the Pentagon Press agent, Sylvester, so brazenly proclaimed that the government has the right to lie to the people. What he really meant was that our CFR controlled government had the power to lie to and be believed by the brain-washed American people.

And let's again go back to the first days of the Illuminati. Because Britain and France were the two greatest world powers in the late years of the 18th Century, Weishaupt ordered the Illuminati to foment the colonial wars, including our Revolutionary War, to weaken the British Empire and organize the French Revolution to destroy the French empire. He scheduled the French Revolution to start in 1789. However, in 1784, a true act of God placed the Bavarian government in possession of evidence which proved the existence of the Illuminati and that evidence could have saved France if they, the French government, hadn't refused to believe it.

Here is how that act of God happened. It was in [1874, says audio, but surely meant] 1784 that Weishaupt issued his orders for the French Revolution. A German writer, named Zwack, put it into book form. It contained the entire Illuminati story and Weishaupt's plans. A copy of this book was sent to the Illuminists in France headed by Robespierre whom Weishaupt had delegated to foment the French Revolution.

The courier was struck and killed by lightening as he rode through Rallestown on his way from Frankfurt to Paris. The police found the subversive documents on his body and turned them over to the proper authorities. After careful study of the plot, the Bavarian government ordered the police to raid Weishaupt's newly organized Lodges of the Grand Orient and the homes of his most influential associates.

All additional evidence thus discovered convinced the authorities that the documents were genuine copies of the conspiracy by which the Illuminati planned to use wars and revolutions to bring about the establishment of a one-world government, the powers of which they, headed by the Rothschilds, intended to usurp as soon as it was established, exactly in line with the United Nations plot of today.

In 1785, the Bavarian government outlawed the Illuminati and closed the Lodges of the Grand Orient. In 1786, they published all the details of the conspiracy. The English title of that publication is *"The Original Writings of the Order and the Sect of the Illuminati."* Copies of the entire conspiracy were sent to all the heads of church and state in Europe. But the power of the Illuminati, which was actually the power of the Rothschilds, was so great that this warning was ignored.

Nevertheless, the Illuminati became a dirty word and it went underground.

At the same time, Weishaupt ordered Illuminists to infiltrate into the Lodges of Blue Masonry and formed their own secret societies within all secret societies. Only Masons who proved themselves internationalists and those whose conduct proved they had defected from God were initiated into the Illuminati. Thenceforth, the conspirators donned the cloak of philanthropy and humanitarianism to conceal their revolutionary and subversive activities.

In order to infiltrate into Masonic Lodges in Britain, Weishaupt invited John Robison over to Europe. Robison was a high degree Mason in the Scottish Rite. He was a professor of natural philosophy at Edinburgh University and Secretary of the Royal Society of Edinburgh. Robison did not fall for the lie that the objective of the Illuminati was to create a benevolent dictatorship, but he kept his reactions to himself so well that he was entrusted with a copy of Weishaupt's revised conspiracy for study and safekeeping.

Anyway, because the heads of state and church in France were deluded into ignoring the warnings given them, the revolution broke out in 1789 as scheduled by Weishaupt. In order to alert other governments to their danger, in 1798, Robison published a book entitled *"Proof of a Conspiracy to Destroy all Governments and Religions"* but his warnings were ignored, exactly as our American people have been ignoring all warnings about the United Nations and the Council on Foreign Relations (the CFR).

[PART 2]

Now here is something that will stun and very likely outrage many who hear this, but there is documentary proof that our own Thomas Jefferson and Alexander Hamilton became students of Weishaupt. Jefferson was one of Weishaupt's strongest defenders when he was outlawed by his government and it was Jefferson who infiltrated the Illuminati into the then newly organized lodges of the Scottish Rite in New England. Here is the proof.

In 1789, John Robison warned all Masonic leaders in America that the Illuminati had infiltrated into their lodges and on July 19, 1789, David Papen, President of Harvard University, issued the same warning to the graduating class and lectured them on the influence of Illuminism was acquiring on American politics and religion, and to top it off, John Quincy Adams, who had organized the New England Masonic Lodges, issued his warnings. He wrote three letters to Colonel William L. Stone, a top Mason, in which he exposed how Jefferson was using Masonic lodges for subversive Illuministic purposes. Those three letters are at this very time in Whittenburg Square Library in Philadelphia. In short, Jefferson, founder of the Democratic Party, was a member of the Illuminati which at least partly accounts for the condition of the party at this time and through infiltration of the Republican Party, we have exactly nothing of loyal Americanism today.

[Audio missing here? It seems an abrupt change of subject!]

That disastrous rebuff at the Congress of Vienna created by the Czar of Russia, Alexander I, did not by any means destroy the Illuminati conspiracy. It merely forced them to adopt a new strategy realizing that the one-world idea was, for the moment, killed, the Rothschild's decided that to keep the plot alive they would have to do it by heightening their control of the money systems of the European nations.

Earlier, by a ruse the outcome of the Battle of Waterloo had been falsified, Rothschild had spread a story that Napoleon had one bad battle. That had precipitated a terrific panic on the stock market in England. All stocks had plummeted down to practically zero and Nathan Rothschild bought all the stocks for virtually a penny on its dollar values.

That gave him complete control of the economy of Britain and virtually of all Europe. So immediately after that Congress in Vienna had boomeranged, Rothschild forced Britain to set up a new Bank of England which he absolutely controlled, exactly as later, through Jacob Schiff, he engineered our own Federal Reserve Act which gave the House of Rothschild a secret control of the economy in the United States. But now for a moment, let's dwell on the activities of the Illuminati in the United States.

In 1826, one Captain William Morgan decided it was his duty to inform all Masons and the general public what the full proof was regarding the Illuminati, their secret plans, and intended objectives; also reveal the identities of the masterminds of the conspiracy. The Illuminati promptly tried Morgan in absentia and convicted him of treason.

They ordered one Richard Howard, an English Illuminist, to carry out their sentence of execution as a traitor. Morgan was warned and he tried to escape to Canada, but Howard caught up with him near the border, near the Niagara Gorge to be exact, where he murdered him. This was verified in a sworn statement made in New York by one Avery Allen to the effect that he heard Howard render his report of the execution to a meeting of Knights Templars in St. John's Hall in New York. He also told how arrangements had been made to ship Howard back to England.

That Allen affidavit is on record in New York City Archives. Very few Masons and very few of the general public know that general disapproval over that incident of murder caused approximately half of all the Masons in the northern jurisdiction of the United States to secede. Copies of the minutes of the meeting held to discuss that matter are still in existence in safe hands and that all that secrecy emphasizes the power of the masterminds of the Illuminati to prevent such terrible events of history from being taught in our schools.

In the early 1850's the Illuminati held a secret meeting in New York which was addressed by a British Illuminist named Wright. Those in attendance were told that the Illuminati was organizing to unite the Nihilist and Atheist groups with all other subversive groups into an international group to be known as Communists. That was when the word *'communist'* first came into being and it was intended to be the supreme weapon and scare word to terrify the whole world and drive the terrorized peoples into the Illuminati one-world scheme.

This scheme, communism, was to be used to enable the Illuminati to foment future wars and revolutions. Clinton Roosevelt (a direct ancestor of Franklin Roosevelt), Horace Greeley, and Charles Dana, foremost newspaper publishers of that time were appointed to head a committee to raise funds for the new venture. Of course, most of the funds were provided by the Rothschilds and this fund was used to finance Karl Marx and Engels when they wrote *"Das Kaptial"* and the *"Communist Manifesto"* in Soho, England. And this clearly reveals that communism is not a so– called ideology, but a secret weapon, a bogy man word to serve the purpose of the Illuminati.

Weishaupt died in 1830, but prior to his death, he prepared a revised version of the age-old conspiracy, the Illuminati, which under various aliases was to organize, finance, direct, and control all international organizations and groups by working their agents into executive positions at the top.

In the United States we have Woodrow Wilson, Franklin Roosevelt, Jack Kennedy, Johnson, Rusk, McNamara, Fulbright, etc., as prime examples.

In addition, while Karl Marx was writing the Communist Manifesto under the direction of one group of Illuminists, Professor Karl Ritter of Frankfurt University was writing the antithesis under direction of another group. The idea was that those who direct the overall conspiracy could use the differences in those two so-called ideologies to enable them to divide larger and larger numbers of the human race into opposing camps so that they could be armed and then brainwashed into fighting and destroying each other, and particularly, to destroy all political and religious institutions.

The work Ritter started was continued after his death and completed by the German so-called philosopher Friedrich Wilhelm Nietzsche who founded *Nietzscheanism*. This Nietzscheanism was later developed into *Fascism* and then into *Nazism* and was used to foment World War I and II.

In 1834 the Italian revolutionary leader,

Guiseppe Mazzini, was selected by the Illuminati to direct their revolutionary program throughout the world. He served in that capacity until he died in 1872, but some years before he died, Mazzini had enticed an American General named Albert Pike into the Illuminati. Pike was fascinated by the idea of a one-world government and ultimately he became the head of this luciferian conspiracy.

Between 1859 and 1871 he, Pike, worked out a military blueprint for three world wars and various revolutions throughout the world which he considered would forward the conspiracy to its final stage in the 20th century. Again I remind that these conspirators were never concerned with immediate success. They also operated on a long-range view.

Pike did most of his work in his home in Little Rock, Arkansas. But a few years later, when the Illuminati's Lodges of the Grand Orient became suspect and repudiated because of Mazzini's revolutionary activities in Europe, Pike organized what he called the *New and Reformed Palladian Right*.

He set up three Supreme Councils: one in Charleston, South Carolina; one in Rome, Italy; and a third in Berlin, Germany. He had Mazzini establish 23 subordinate councils in strategic locations throughout the world. These have been the secret headquarters of the world revolutionary movement ever since.

Long before Marconi invented radio, the scientists in the Illuminati had found the means for Pike and the heads of his councils to communicate secretly. It was the discovery of that secret that enabled intelligence officers to understand how apparently unrelated incidents, ones such as the assassination of an Austrian Prince at Sarajevo, took place simultaneously throughout the world which developed into a war or a revolution.

Pike's plan was as simple as it has proved effective. It called for Communism, Nazism, political Zionism, and other international movements be organized and used to foment three global world wars and at least two major revolutions.

The first world war was to be fought so as to enable the Illuminati to destroy Czarism in Russia, as vowed by Rothschild after the Czar had torpedoed his scheme at the Congress in Vienna, and to transform Russia into a stronghold of atheistic communism. The differences stirred up by agents of the Illuminati between the British and German Empires were to be used to foment this war. After the war would be ended, communism was to be built up and used to destroy other governments and weaken religions.

World War II, when and if necessary, was to be fomented by using the controversies between Fascists and political zionists, and here let it be noted that Hitler was financed by Krupp, the

Warburgs, the Rothschilds, and other internationalist bankers and that the slaughter of the supposed 600,000 Jews by Hitler didn't bother the Jewish internationalist bankers at all.

That slaughter was necessary in order to create worldwide hatred of the German people and thus bring about the war against them. In short, this second world war was to be fought to destroy nazism and to increase the power of political zionism so that the state of Israel could be established in Palestine.

During this World War II, international communism was to be built up until it equalled in strength to that of united Christendom. When it reached that point, it was to be contained and kept in check until required for the final social cataclysm. As we know now, Roosevelt, Churchill, and Stalin put that exact policy into effect and Truman, Eisenhower, Kennedy, and Johnson continued that same exact policy.

World War III is to be fomented by using the so-called controversies, the agents of the Illuminati operating under whatever new name, are now being stored up between the political Zionists and the leaders of the Moslem world. That war is to be directed in such a manner that all of Islam and political Zionism (Israel) will destroy each other while at the same time, the remaining nations once more divided on this issue will be forced to fight themselves into a state of complete exhaustion –

physically, mentally, spiritually, and economically.

Now, can any thinking person doubt that the intrigue now going on in the Near-, Middle-, and Far – East is designed to accomplish that satanic objective? Pike himself foretold all this in a statement he made to Mazzini on August 15, 1871. Pike stated that after World War III is ended, those who will inspire to undisputed world domination will provoke the greatest social cataclysm the world has ever known. Quoting his own words taken from the letter he wrote to Mazzini and which letter is now catalogued in the British Museum in London, England, he said:

> "We shall unleash the nihilists and the atheists and we shall provoke a great social cataclysm which in all its horror will show clearly to all nations the effect of absolute atheism, the origins of savagery and of most bloody turmoil. Then everywhere, the people forced to defend themselves against the world minority of the world revolutionaries and will exterminate those destroyers of civilization and the multitudes disillusioned with Christianity whose deistic spirits will be from that moment on without direction and leadership and anxious for an ideal, but without knowledge where to send its adoration, will receive the true light through the universal manifestation of the pure doctrine of Lucifer brought finally out into public view. A manifestation which will result from a general reactionary movement which will follow the destruction of Christianity and Atheism; both conquered and exterminated at the same time."

When Mazzini died in 1872, Pike made another Italian revolutionary leader named Adrian Lemmy, his successor. Lemmy, in turn, was succeeded by Lenin and Trotsky, then by Stalin. The revolutionary activities of all those men were financed by British, French, German, and American international bankers – all of them dominated by the House of Rothschilds.

We are supposed to believe that the international bankers of today, like the money changers of Christ's day, are only the tools or agents of the great conspiracy, but actually they are the masterminds behind all of it, while the general public has been brain-washed by all the mass communications media into believing that communism is a movement of the so-called workers. The actual fact is that both British and American intelligence officers have authentic documentary evidence that international liberals, operating through their international banking houses, particularly the House of Rothschilds, have financed both sides of every war and revolution since 1776.

Those who today comprise the conspiracy (the CFR in the United States) direct our governments whom they hold in usury through such methods as the Federal Reserve System in America to fight wars, such as Vietnam (created by the United Nations), so as to further Pike's Illuminati plans to bring the world to that stage of the conspiracy when atheistic communism and the whole of Christianity can be forced into an all out third world war within each remaining nation as well as on an international scale.

The headquarters of the great conspiracy in the late 1700's was in Frankfurt, Germany where the House of Rothschild had been established by Mayer Anselm who adopted the Rothschild name and linked together other international financiers who had literally sold their souls to the devil. After the Bavarian government's exposure in 1786, the conspirators moved their headquarters to Switzerland then to London. Since World War II, after Jacob Schiff, the Rothschild's boy in America died, the headquarters of the American branch has been in the Harold Pratt Building in New York, and the Rockefellers, originally proteges of Schiff, have taken over the manipulation of finances in America for the Illuminati.

In the final phases of the conspiracy, the one-world government will consist of the king-dictator, head of the United Nations, the CFR, and a few billionaires, economists, and scientists who have proved their devotion to the great conspiracy. All others are to be integrated into a vast conglomeration of mongrelized humanity – actually slaves.

Now let me show you how our federal government and the American people have been sucked into the one-world take-over plot of the Illuminati great conspiracy and always bear in mind, that the United Nations was created to become the housing for that one-world, so-called, liberal conspiracy. The real foundations of the plot of the takeover of the United States were laid during the period of our Civil War. Not that Weishaupt and the earlier masterminds had ever overlooked the new world, as I have previously indicated, Weishaupt had his agents planted over here as far back as the Revolutionary War. But George Washington was more than a match for them.

It was during the Civil War that the conspirators launched their first concrete efforts. We know that Judah Benjamin, chief advisor of Jefferson Davis, was a Rothschild agent. We also know that there were Rothschild agents planted in Abraham Lincoln's cabinet who tried to sell him into a financial dealing with the House of Rothschild.

But old Abe saw through the scheme and bluntly rejected it thereby incurring the undying enmity of the Rothschilds, exactly as the Russian Czar did when he torpedoed their first League of Nations at the Congress in Vienna. Investigation of the assassination of Lincoln revealed that the assassin, Booth, was a member of a secret conspiratorial group. Because there were a number of highly important government officials involved, the name of the group was never revealed and it became a mystery, exactly as the assassination of Jack Kennedy still is a mystery. But I am sure it will not for long remain a mystery.

Anyway, the ending of the Civil War destroyed, temporarily, all chances of the House of Rothschilds to get a clutch on our money system, such as they had acquired in Britain and other nations in Europe. I say temporarily because the Rothschilds and the masterminds of the conspiracy never quit, so they had to start from scratch. But they lost no time in getting started.

Shortly after the Civil War, a young immigrant, who called himself Jacob H. Schiff, arrived in New York. Jacob was a young man with a mission for the House of Rothschild. Jacob was the son of a Rabbi born in one of the Rothschild's houses in Frankfurt, Germany.

I won't go deeply into his background. The important point was that Rothschild recognized in him not only a potential money wizard, but more important, he also saw the latent Machiavellian qualities in Jacob that could, as it did, make him an invaluable functionary in the great one-world conspiracy.

After a comparatively brief training period in the Rothschild's London Bank, Jacob left for America with instructions to buy into a banking house which was to be the springboard to acquire control of the money system of the United States. Actually, Jacob came here to carry out four specific assignments:

1. And most important, was to acquire

control of America's money system.

2.   Find desirable men, who for a price, would be willing to serve as stooges for the great conspiracy and promote them into high places in our federal government, our Congress, and the US Supreme Court, and all federal agencies.

3.   Create minority group strife throughout the nations – particularly between the whites and blacks.

4.   Create a movement to destroy religion in the United States, but Christianity to be the chief target.

[PART 3]

[1. Take control of US money system.]

E arlier I stated that Jacob Schiff came to America with orders by Rothschild to carry out four specific directives. The first and most important one was to get control of the United States' money system. Let's trace Schiff's step to accomplish that directive. As a first step he had to buy into a banking house, but it had to be the kind of a house that he could absolutely control and mold for that primary objective of entrapping our US money system.

After carefully scouting around, Jacob bought a partnership in a firm that called itself *Kuhn and Loeb*. Like Schiff, Kuhn and Loeb were immigrants from German Jewish ghettos. They came to the United States in the mid 1840's. Both started their business careers as itinerant pack peddlers. In the early 1850's they pooled their interests and set up a merchandise store in Lafayette, Indiana under the firm name of *Kuhn and Loeb* servicing the covered wagon settlers on their way west. In the years that followed, they set up similar stores in Cincinnati and St. Louis. Then they added pawnbroking to their merchandising pursuits. From that to money lending was a short and quick step.

By the time Schiff arrived on the scene, *Kuhn and Loeb* was a well-known private banking firm, and this is the firm Jacob bought into. Shortly after he became a partner in *Kuhn and Loeb*, Schiff married Loeb's daughter, Teresa, then he bought out Kuhn's interests and moved the firm to New York and *Kuhn and Loeb* became *Kuhn-Loeb & Company*; international bankers with Jacob Schiff, agent of the Rothschilds, ostensibly the sole owner. And throughout his career, this blend of Judas and Machiavelli, the first hierarch of the Illuminati's great conspiracy in America, posed as a generous philanthropist and a man of great holiness – the cover-up policy set forth by the Illuminati.

[2. Install puppets in government.]

As I have stated, the first great step of the conspiracy was to be the entrapment of our money system. To achieve that objective, Schiff had to get full cooperation of the then big banker elements in America, and that was easier said than done. Even in those years, Wall Street was the heart of the American money mart and J.P. Morgan was its dictator. Next in line were the Drexels and the Biddles of Philadelphia. All the other financiers, big and little, danced to the music of those three houses, but particularly to that of Morgan. All of those three were proud, haughty, arrogant potentates.

For the first few years, they viewed the little bewhiskered man from the German ghettos with utter contempt, but Jacob knew how to overcome that. He threw a few Rothschild bones to them. Said bones being distribution in America of desirable European stock and bond issues. Then he discovered that he had a still more potent weapon in his hands in the following:

It was in the decades following our Civil War that our industries began to burgeon. We had great railroads to build. The oil, mining, steel, textile industries were bursting out of their swaddling clothes. All of that called for vast financing. Much of that financing had to come from abroad. That meant the House of Rothschild and that was when Schiff came into his own. He played a very crafty game.

He became the patron saint of John D. Rockefeller, Edward R. Harriman, and Andrew Carnegie. He financed the Standard Oil Company for Rocky, the Railroad Empire for Harriman, and the Steel Empire for Carnegie. But instead of hogging all the other industries for Kuhn-Loeb & Company, he opened the doors of the House of Rothschild to Morgan, Biddle, and Drexel. In turn, Rothschild arranged the setting up of London, Paris, European and other branches for those three, but always in partnerships with Rothschild subordinates and Rothschild made it very clear to all those men that Schiff was to be the boss in New York.

Thus at the turn of the century Schiff had a tight control of the entire banking fraternity on Wall Street which by then, with Schiff's help, included Lehman brothers, Goldman-Sachs, and other internationalist banks headed by men chosen by the Rothschilds. In short, that meant control of the nation's money powers and he was then ready for the giant step – the entrapment of our national money system.

Now under our Constitution, all control of our money system is vested solely in our Congress. Schiff's next important step was to seduce our Congress to betray that Constitutional edict by surrendering that control to the hierarchy of the Illuminati's great conspiracy. In order to legalize that surrender and thus make the people powerless to resist it, it would be necessary to have Congress enact special legislation.

To accomplish that, Schiff would have to infiltrate stooges into both houses of Congress. Stooges powerful enough to railroad Congress into passing such legislation. Equally, or even more important, he would have to plant a stooge in the White House a president that is without integrity and without scruples who would sign that legislation into law. To accomplish that, he had to get control of either the Republican or the Democratic Party.

The Democratic Party was the more vulnerable. It was the hungrier of the two parties. Except for Grover Cleveland, the Democrats had been unable to land one of their men in the White House since before the Civil War. There were two reasons for that:

1. Poverty of the Party.
2. There were considerably more Republican-minded voters than Democrats.

The poverty matter was not a great problem, but the voter problem was a different story. But as I previously said, Schiff was a smart cookie.

Here is the atrocious and murderous method he employed to solve that voter problem. His solution emphasizes how very little the Jewish internationalist bankers care about their own racial brethren as you shall see.

Suddenly, around 1890, there broke out a nationwide series of pogroms in Russia. Many, many, thousands of innocent Jews – men, women, and children, were slaughtered by the Cossacks and other peasants. Similar pogroms with similar slaughter of innocent Jews broke out in Poland, Rumania, and Bulgaria. All those pogroms were fomented by Rothschild agents. As a result, Jewish terrified refugees from all of those nations swarmed into the United States and that continued throughout the next two or three decades because the pogroms were continuous through all those years. All those refugees were aided by self-styled humanitarian committees set up by Schiff, the Rothschilds, and all the Rothschild affiliates.

In the main, the refugees streamed into New York, but the Schiff-Rothschild humanitarian committees found ways to shuffle many of them into other large cities such as Chicago, Boston, Philadelphia, Detroit, Los Angeles, etc. All of them were quickly transformed into naturalized citizens and educated to register as Democrats. Thus all of that so-called minority group became solid Democratic voter blocks in their communities, all controlled and maneuvered by their so-called benefactors. And shortly after the turn of the century, they became vital factors in the political life of our nation. That was one of the methods Schiff employed to plant men like Nelson Aldrich in our Senate and Woodrow Wilson in the White House.

[3. Racial Strife.]

At this point let me remind you of another of the important jobs that was assigned to Schiff when he was dispatched to America. I refer to the job of destroying the unity of the American people by creating minority-group and racial strife. By the pogrom-driven Jewish refugees into America, Schiff was creating one ready-made minority group for that purpose. But the Jewish people, as a whole, made fearful by the pogroms, could not be depended upon to create the violence necessary to destroy the unity of the American people.

But right within America, there was an already made-to-order, although as yet a sleeping minority group, the Negroes, who could be sparked into so-called demonstrations, rioting, looting, murder, and every other type of lawlessness. All that was necessary, was to incite and arouse them. Together, those two minority groups, properly maneuvered, could be used to create exactly the kind of strife in America the Illuminati would need to accomplish their objective.

Thus at the same time that Schiff and co-conspirators were laying their plans for the entrapment of our money system, they were also perfecting plans to hit the unsuspecting American people with an explosive and terrifying racial upheaval that would tear the people into hate-factions and create chaos throughout the nation, especially on all college and university campuses, all protected by Earl Warren decisions and our so-called leaders in Washington. Of course, perfecting those plans required time and infinitely patient organizing.

Now to remove all doubts, I take a few moments to give you documentary proof of this racial strife plot. First of all they had to create leadership and organizations to draw in millions of dupes, both Jewish and Negroes, who would do the demonstrating and commit the rioting, looting, and lawlessness.

So in 1909, Schiff, the Lehmans, and other conspirators, organized and set up the *"National Association for the Advancement of the Colored People"* known as the NAACP. The presidents, directors, and legal councils of the NAACP were always white men, Jews, appointed by Schiff, and this is the case to this very day.

Then in 1913, the Schiff group organized the Anti-Defamation League of the B'nai B'rith commonly known as the ADL to serve as the gestapo and hatchet-man outfit for the entire great conspiracy.

Today this sinister ADL maintains over 2,000 agencies in all parts of the country and they advise and completely control every action of the NAACP or of the Urban League of all the other so-called Negro civil rights organizations throughout the nation including such leaders as Martin 'Lucifer' King, Stockely Carmichael, Bayard Rustin, and others of that ilk.

In addition, the ADL acquired absolute control of the advertising budgets of many department-stores, hotel-chains, and TV and Radio industrialist sponsors, also advertising-agencies in order to control practically all the mass-communications media and force every loyal newspaper to slant and falsify the news and to further incite, and, at the same time create sympathy for, the lawlessness and violence of the Negro mobs.

Here is documentary proof of the beginning of their deliberate plot to foment the Negroes into all their lawlessness:

Around 1910, one Israel Zengwill wrote a play entitled *"The Melting-Pot"*. It was sheer propaganda to incite the Negroes and Jews because the play purportedly visualized how the American people were discriminating against, and persecuting Jews and Negroes. At that time nobody seemed to realize that it was a propaganda play – it was that cleverly-written. The propaganda was well wrapped up in the true, great entertainment in the play, and it was a big Broadway Hit.

Now in those years, the legendary Diamond Jim Brady used to throw a banquet at the famous Delmonico Restaurant in New York after the opening-performance of a popular play. He threw such a party for the cast of *"The Melting-Pot"*, its author, producer, and chosen Broadway celebrities. By then I'd already made a personal mark on the Broadway Theater and was invited to that party. There I met George Bernard Shaw and a Jewish writer named Israel Cohen. Zangwill, Shaw, and Cohen were the triumvirate who created the Fabian Society in England and had worked closely with a Frankfurt Jew named Mordicai who had changed his name to Karl Marx, but remember, at that time both Marxism and Communism were just emerging and nobody paid much attention to either, and nobody suspected the propaganda in the writings of those three really brilliant writers.

At that banquet, Israel Cohen told me that he was then engaged in writing a book which was to be a follow-up on Zangwill's *"The Melting-Pot"*. The title of his book was to be *"A Racial Program for the 20th Century."* At that time I was completely absorbed by my work as a playwright, and significant as that title was, its real objective never dawned on me nor was I interested in reading the book. But it suddenly hit me with the force of a hydrogen bomb when I received a newspaper clipping of an item published by the Washington D.C. *Evening Star* in May 1957. That item was a verbatim reprint of the following excerpt in Israel Cohen's book "A Racial Program for the 20th Century" and it reads as I quote:

"We must realize that our party's most powerful weapon is racial tension. By propounding into the consciousness of the dark races, that for centuries they have been oppressed by the whites, we can move them to the program of the communist party. In America, we will aim for subtle victory. While inflaming the Negro minority against the whites, we will instill in the whites a guilt-complex for their exploitation of the Negroes. We will aid the Negroes to rise to prominence in every walk of life, in the professions, and in the world of sports and entertainment. With this prestige, the Negro will be able to intermarry with the whites and begin a process which will deliver America to our cause."

That same excerpt was entered into the Congressional Record of June 7, 1957, by Representative Thomas G. Abernathy. Thus the authenticity of that passage in Cohen's book was fully established. But the one question that remained in my mind was whether it represented the official policy or plot of the Communist Party or just a personal expression of Cohen himself. Hence I sought more proof and I found it in an official pamphlet published in 1935 by the New York Communist Party's official Workers' Library Publishers. That pamphlet was entitled The Negroes in a Soviet America. It urged the Negroes to rise up, form a soviet-state in the south, and apply for admission to the Soviet Union. It contained a firm pledge that the revolt would be supported by all American 'reds' and all so-called liberals. On page 38, it promised that a Soviet government would confer greater benefits to Negroes than to whites and again this official communist pamphlet pledged that, I quote: *"any act of discrimination or prejudice against a Negro will become a crime under the revolutionary law."* That statement proved that the excerpt in Israel Cohen's book published in 1913 was an official edict of the Communist Party and directly in line with the Illuminati blueprint for world revolution issued by Weishaupt and later by Albert Pike.

Now there's only one question and that is to prove that the communist regime is directly

controlled by the American Jacob Schiff and
London Rothschild masterminds of the great
conspiracy. A little later I will provide that proof
that will remove even a remote doubt that the
Communist Party, as we know it, was created by
those masterminds, capitalists if you will note, that
Schiff, the Warburgs, and the Rothschilds planned
and financed the entire Russian Revolution, also the
murder of the Czar and his family, and that Lenin,
Trotsky, and Stalin took their orders directly from
Schiff and the other capitalists whom they
supposedly are fighting.

Now can you see why the vile Earl Warren and
his equally vile co-Supreme Court justices issued
that infamous and treasonous desegregation
decision in 1954? It was to aid and abet the plot of
the Illuminati conspirators to create tension and
strife between the Negroes and Whites. Can you see
why the same Earl Warren issued his decision
prohibiting Christian prayers and Christmas carols
in our schools? It was done to destroy Christianity.
Can you see why Eisenhower, despite all the rigid
constitutional prohibitions, sent federal troops into
a southern state to enforce the desegregation
decision? Why Kennedy did likewise? And can you
see why Johnson and 66 Senators, despite the
protests of 90% of the American people, voted for
the *Consular Treaty* which opens our entire country
to Russian spies and saboteurs? All those 66
Senators are 20th century 'Benedict Arnolds'.

It is up to you and you, all of the American

people, to force Congress, our elected servants, to haul in those American traitors for impeachments and that when proven guilty, they all be given the punishment prescribed for traitors who aid and abet our enemies. And that includes the forcing of rigid investigations by Congress of the CFR and all their fronts, such as the ADL, the NAACP, SNIC, and such Illuminati tools as Martin 'Lucifer' King. Such investigations will completely unmask all the leaders in Washington and the Illuminati and all their affiliations and affiliates as traitors carrying out the Illuminati plot. It will completely unmask the United Nations as the intended crux of the entire plot and force Congress to take the US out of the UN and hurl the UN out of the US. In fact, it will destroy the UN and the entire plot.

Before I close this phase, I wish to reiterate and stress one vital point which I urge you to never forget if you wish to save our country for your children and their children. Here is the point. Every unconstitutional and unlawful act committed by Woodrow Wilson, by Franklin Roosevelt, by Truman, Eisenhower, and Kennedy and are now being committed by Johnson, is exactly in line with the Illuminati conspirators centuries-old plot outlined by Weishaupt and Albert Pike. Every vicious decision issued by the traitorous Earl Warren and his equally traitorous Supreme Court justices was directly in line with what the Illuminati blueprint required. That all the treason committed by our State Department under Rusk and earlier by John Foster Dulles, and Marshall, also all the treason committed by McNamara and his predecessors is directly in line with that same Illuminati blueprint for the takeover of the world. Also the amazing treason by various members of our Congress, especially by the 66 Senators who signed for the Consular Treaty, has been committed on orders from the Illuminati.

[PART 4]

Now I will go back to Jacob Schiff's entrapment of our money system and the treasonous actions that followed. It will also reveal the Schiff-Rothschild control of not only Karl Marx, but of Lenin, Trotsky, and Stalin, who created the revolution in Russia and set up the Communist Party.

It was in 1908 that Schiff decided that the time had come for his seizure of our money system. His chief lieutenants in that seizure were Colonel Edward Mandell House whose entire career was that of chief executive and courier for Schiff as I shall show, Bernard Barouk, and Herbert Lehman. In the fall of that year, they assembled in secret conclave at the Jekyll Island Hunt Club, owned by J.P. Morgan at Jekyll Island, Georgia. Among those present were J.P. Morgan, John D. Rockefeller, Colonel House, Senator Nelson Aldrich, Schiff, Stillman and Vandlelip of the New York National City Bank, W. and J. Seligman, Eugene Myer, Bernard Barouk, Herbert Lehman, Paul Warburg, in short, all of the international bankers in America. All of them members of the hierarchy of the Illuminati's great conspiracy.

A week later they emerged with what they

called the Federal Reserve System. Senator Aldrich was the stooge who was to railroad it through Congress, but they held that railroading in abeyance for one chief reason. They would first have to plant their man, an obedient stooge, in the White House to sign the Federal Reserve Act into law. They knew that even if the Senate would pass that act unanimously, the then newly elected President Taft would promptly veto it. So they waited.

In 1912, *their* man, Woodrow Wilson, was elected to the presidency. Immediately after Wilson was inaugurated, Senator Aldrich railroaded the Federal Reserve Act through both houses of Congress and Wilson promptly signed it and the Federal Reserve Act became law. That heinous act of treason was committed on December 23, 1913, two days before Christmas when all the members of Congress, except for several carefully picked Representatives and three equally carefully picked Senators, were away from Washington. How heinous treasonous was that act? I'll tell you. Our founding fathers knew full well the power of money. They knew that whoever had that power held the destiny of our nation in his hands. Therefore, they carefully guarded this power when they set forth in the Constitution, that Congress, the elected representatives of the people, alone would have the power. The Constitutional language on this point is brief, concise, and specific, stated in Article I, Section 8, Paragraph 5, defining the duties and powers of Congress, and I quote: *"to coin money, regulate the value thereof, and of foreign coin, and the standard of weights and measures."* But on that tragic, unforgettable day of infamy, December 23, 1913, the men we sent to Washington to safeguard our interests, the Representatives and Senators and Woodrow Wilson, delivered the destiny of our nation into the hands of two aliens from Eastern Europe, Jacob Schiff and Paul Warburg. Warburg was a very recent immigrant who came here on orders from Rothschild for the express purpose of blueprinting that foul Federal Reserve Act.

Now the vast majority of the American people think that the Federal Reserve System is the United States Government owned agency. That is positively false. All of the stock of the federal reserve banks is owned by the member banks and the heads of the member banks are all members of the hierarchy of the great Illuminati conspiracy known today as the CFR.

The details of that act of treason, in which many traitorous so-called Americans participated, are far too long for this reporting, but all those details are available in a book entitled, *"The Federal Reserve Conspiracy"*, written by Eustace Mullins. In that book, Mullins tells the entire horrifying story and backs it up with unquestionable documentations. Aside from it being a truly fascinating and shocking story of that great betrayal, every American should read it as a matter of vital intelligence for the time when the whole American people will finally come awake and smash the entire conspiracy and with God's help, that awakening will surely come. You can get a copy of that book from the publisher, The Christian Educational Association, 530 Chestnut St., Union, New Jersey.

Now if you think that those aliens and their by accident-of-birth American co-conspirators would be content with just the control of our money system, you are in for another very sad shock. The Federal Reserve System gave the conspirators complete control of our money system, but it in no way touched the earnings of the people because the Constitution positively forbids what is now known as the 20% withholding tax. But the Illuminati blueprint for one-world enslavement called for the confiscation of all private property and control of individual earning powers. This, and Karl Marx stressed that feature in his blueprint, had to be accomplished by a progressive graduated income tax. As I have stated, such a tax could not lawfully be imposed upon the American people. It is succinctly and expressly forbidden by our Constitution. Thus, only an Amendment to the Constitution could give the federal government such confiscatory powers.

Well, that too was not an insurmountable problem for our Machiavellian plotters. The same elected leaders in both houses of Congress and the same Mr. Woodrow Wilson, who signed the infamous Federal Reserve Act into law, amended the Constitution to make the federal income tax, known as the 16th Amendment, a law of the land. Both are illegal under our Constitution. In short, the same traitors signed both betrayals, the Federal Reserve Act and the 16th Amendment, into law. However, it seems that nobody ever realized that the 16th amendment was set up to rob, and I do mean rob, the people of their earnings via the income tax provision.

The plotters didn't fully use the provision until World War II when that great humanitarian, Franklin Roosevelt, applied a 20% withholding tax on all small wage earners and up to 90% on higher incomes. Oh, of course, he faithfully promised that it would be only for the duration of the war, but what was a promise to such a charlatan who in 1940, when he was running for his third term, kept proclaiming: *"I say again and again and again that I will never send American boys to fight on foreign soil."* Remember? He was proclaiming that even as he was already preparing to plunge us into World War II by enticing the Japanese into that 'sneak attack' on Pearl Harbor to furnish him with his excuse.

And before I forget, let me remind you that another charlatan named Woodrow Wilson used exactly that same campaign slogan in 1916. His slogan was, *"Re-elect the man who will keep your sons out of the war."* Exactly the same formula, exactly the same promises. But wait, as Al Jolson used to say, *"You ain't heard nothin' yet."* That 16th Amendment income tax trap was intended to confiscate – rob – the earnings only of the common herd, you and me. It was not intended to even touch the huge incomes of the Illuminati gang, the Rockefellers, the Carnegies, the Lehmans, and all the other conspirators.

So together, with that 16th Amendment, they created what they called the tax-free foundations that would enable the conspirators to transform their huge wealth into such so-called foundations and avoid payment of virtually all income taxes. The excuse for it was that the earnings of those tax-free foundations would be devoted to humanitarian philanthropy. So we now have the several Rockefeller Foundations, the Carnegie Endowment Fund, the Ford Foundation, the Mellon Foundation, and hundreds of similar tax-free foundations.

And what kind of philanthropy do these foundations support? Well, they finance all the civil rights groups that are creating all the chaos and rioting all over the country. They finance the Martin 'Lucifer' Kings. The Ford Foundation finances the Center for the Study of Democratic Institutions in Santa Barbara, commonly referred to as Moscow West, and which is headed by 'wonder boy' Hutchens, Walter Ruther, Erwin Canham and others of that ilk.

In short, the tax-free foundations financed those who are doing the job for the Illuminati's great conspiracy. And what are the hundreds of billions of dollars they confiscate every year from the earnings of the common herd, you and me, used for? Well, for one thing, there is the foreign aid gimmick which gave billions to communist Tito, plus gifts of hundreds of jet planes, many of which were turned over to Castro, plus the costs of training communist pilots so that they can the better to shoot down our planes. Billions to red Poland. Billions to India. Billions to Sukarno. Billions to other enemies of the United States. That's what that treasonously railroaded 16th Amendment has done to our nation, to the American people, to you and to me, to your children and their children.

Our CFR Illuminati controlled federal government can grant tax-free status to all foundations and pro-red one-world outfits, such as the Fund for the Republic. But if you or a patriotic pro- organization is too outspokenly pro-American, they can terrify and intimidate you by finding a misplaced comma in your income-tax report and by threatening you with penalties, fines, and even prison. Future historians will wonder how the American people could have been so naive and stupid as to have permitted such audacious brazen acts of treason as the Federal Reserve Act and the 16th Amendment. Well, they were not naive and they were not stupid. The answer is, they trusted the men they elected to safeguard our country and our people, and they just didn't have even an inkling about either betrayal, until after each one had been accomplished.

It was the Illuminati controlled mass communications media that kept, and is keeping, our people naive and stupid and unaware of the treason being committed. Now the great question is, when will the people wake up and do to our traitors of today what George Washington and our founding fathers would have done to Benedict Arnold? Actually, Benedict Arnold was a petty traitor compared to our present traitors in Washington. Now let's go back to the events that followed the rape of our Constitution by the passage of the Federal Reserve Act and the 16th Amendment. Was Wilson completely under their control?

The masterminds of the great conspiracy put in motion their next and what they hoped would be their final steps to achieve their one-world government. The first of those steps was to be World War I. Why War? Simple. The only excuse for a one-world government was that it will supposedly ensure peace. The only thing that can make people cry for peace, is war. War brings chaos, destruction, exhaustion, to winner as well as to loser. It brings economic ruin to both. Most important, it destroys the flower of the young manhood of both. To the saddened and heartbroken oldsters the mothers and fathers who are left with nothing but memories of their beloved sons, peace becomes worth any price. And that is the emotion upon which the conspirators depend for the success of their satanic plot.

Throughout the 19th century, from 1814 to 1914, the world, as a whole, was at peace. Such wars as the Franco-Prussian, our own Civil War, the Russo-Japanese War, were what might be termed local disturbances that did not affect the rest of the world. All the great nations were prosperous and the people staunchly nationalistic and fiercely proud of their sovereignties. It was utterly unthinkable that the French and the German peoples would be willing to live under a one-world government, or the Turks and the Russians, or the Chinese and the Japanese. Even more unthinkable is that a Kaiser Wilhelm, or a Franz Joseph, or a Czar Nicholas, or any Monarch, would willingly and meekly surrender his throne to a one-world government. But bear in mind that the peoples in all nations are the real power and only one thing, war, could make the peoples yearn and clamor for a peace- ensuring one-world government. But it would have to be a frightful and horribly devastating war. It could not be just a local disturbing war between just two nations, it would have to be a world war.

No major nation must be left untouched by the horrors and devastation of such a war. The cry for peace must be made universal.

Actually that was the format set by the Illuminati and Nathan Rothschild at the turn of the 19th century. They first maneuvered all of Europe into the Napoleonic Wars, then the Congress in Vienna which they, and particularly Rothschild, planned to transform into a League of Nations which was to have been the housing for their one-world government, exactly as the present United Nations was set up to be the housing for the forthcoming, God forbid, one-world government.

Anyway, that was the format the House of Rothschild and Jacob Schiff decided to employ to achieve their objective in 1914. Of course they knew that the same format had failed in 1814, but they theorized, that this was only because the Czar of Russia had torpedoed that scheme. Well, the present 1914 conspirators would eliminate that 1814 'fly in the ointment'. They'd make sure that after the new world war that they were conspiring, there'd be no Czar of Russia around to throw monkey-wrenches into the machinery.

I won't go into how they accomplished this first step to launch a world war. History records that World War I was precipitated by a trivial incident, the kind of incident both Weishaupt and Albert Pike had incorporated in their blueprints. That incident was the assassination of an Austrian Archduke arranged by the Illuminati masterminds. The war followed. It involved Germany, Austria, Hungary, and their allies (so-called the Axis powers), against France, Britain, and Russia, called the Allies. Only the United States was *not* involved during the first two years.

By 1917 the conspirators had achieved their primary objective. All of Europe was in a state of destitution. All the peoples were war weary and crying for 'peace'. And the outcome too was all set. It was to come as soon as the United States would be hurled on the side of the Allies, and that was all set to happen immediately after Wilson's re-election. After that, there could be only one outcome.

Complete victory for the Allies. To fully confirm my statement that long before 1917, the conspiracy, headed in America by Jacob Schiff, had it all set to hurl the United States into that war, I will cite the proof:

When Wilson was campaigning for re-election in 1916, his chief appeal was *"re-elect the man who will keep your sons out of the war."* But during that same campaign, the Republican Party publicly charged that Wilson had long committed himself to throw us into the war. They charged that if he would be defeated he would accomplish that act during his few remaining months in office, but if re-elected, he would hold off until after re-election. But at that time the American people looked upon Wilson as a God-man. Well, Wilson was re-elected and as per the schedule of the conspirators, he hurled us into the war in 1917. He used the sinking of the *Lusitania* as an excuse – a sinking which also was prearranged. Roosevelt, also a God-man in the eyes of the American people, followed the same technique in 1941 when he used the prearranged Pearl Harbor attack as his excuse for hurling us into World War II.

Now exactly as the conspirators planned, victory for the Allies would eliminate all the Monarchs of the defeated Nations and leave all their peoples leaderless, confused, bewildered, and perfectly conditioned for the one-world government the great conspiracy intended would follow. But there still would be an obstacle, the same obstacle that had balked the Illuminati and Rothschild at that Congress in Vienna 'peace gathering' after the Napoleonic Wars.

Russia would be on the winning side this time as it was in 1814 and therefore the Czar would be securely on his throne. Here it is pertinent to note that Russia, under the Czarist regime, had been the one country in which the Illuminati had never made any headway nor had the Rothschilds ever been able to infiltrate in their banking interests thus a winning Czar would be more difficult than ever to cope with. Even if he could be enticed into a so-called League of Nations, it was a foregone conclusion that he would never, but never, go for a one-world government.

So even before the outbreak of World War I, the conspirators had a plan in the making to carry out Nathan Rothschild's vow of 1814 to destroy the Czar and also murder all possible royal heirs to the throne and it would have to be done before the close of the war. And the Russian Bolsheviki were to be their instruments in this particular plot. From the turn of the century, the chiefs of the Bolsheviki were Nicolai Lenin, Leon Trotsky, and later Joseph Stalin.

Of course, those were not their true family names. Prior to the outbreak of the war, Lenin headquartered in Paris. After the outbreak,

Switzerland became his haven. Trotsky's headquarters was on the lower East Side in New York, largely the habitat of Russian-Jewish refugees. Both Lenin and Trotsky were similarly bewhiskered and unkempt. In those days, that was the badge of Bolshevism. Both lived well yet neither had a regular occupation.

Neither had any visible means of support, yet both always had plenty of money. All those mysteries were solved in 1917. Right from the outset of the war, strange and mysterious goings-on were taking place in New York. Night after night, Trotsky darted furtively in and out of Jacob Schiff's palatial mansion. And in the dead of those same nights there were a gathering of hoodlums of New York's lower east side – all of them Russian refugees at Trotsky's headquarters, and all were going through some mysterious sort of training process that was all shrouded in mystery. Nobody talked, although it did leak out that Schiff was financing all of Trotsky's activities.

Then suddenly Trotsky vanished. So did approximately 300 of his trained hoodlums. Actually they were on the high seas in a Schiff-chartered ship bound for a rendezvous with Lenin and his gang in Switzerland. And on that ship was $20 million in gold. The $20 million Schiff provided to finance the Bolsheviki takeover of Russia. In anticipation of Trotsky's arrival, Lenin prepared to throw a party in his Switzerland hideaway.

Men of the very highest places in the world were to be guests at that party. Among them were the mysterious Colonel Edward Mandell House, Woodrow Wilson's mentor and palsy-walsy, and more important, Schiff's special and confidential messenger. Another of the expected guests was Warburg, of the Warburg Banking Clan in Germany who was financing the Kaiser and whom the Kaiser had rewarded by making him chief of the Secret Police of Germany. In addition, there were the Rothschilds of London and Paris, also Lithenoth, Kakonavich, and Stalin (who was then the head of a train and bank robbing gang of bandits). He was known as the 'Jesse James of the Urals'.

And here I must remind you that England and France were then long in the war with Germany and that on February 3, 1917, Wilson had broken off all diplomatic relations with Germany. Therefore, Warburg, Colonel House, the Rothschilds, and all those others were enemies, but of course, Switzerland was neutral ground where enemies could meet and be friends, especially if they had some scheme in common.

That Lenin party was very nearly wrecked by an unforeseen incident. The Schiff-chartered ship on its way to Switzerland was intercepted and taken into custody by a British warship. But Schiff quickly rushed orders to Wilson to order the British to release the ship intact with the Trotsky hoodlums and the gold. Wilson obeyed. He warned the British that if they refused to release the ship, the United

States would not enter the war in April as he had faithfully promised a year earlier.

The British headed the warning. Trotsky arrived in Switzerland and the Lenin party went off as scheduled. But they still faced what ordinarily would have been the insurmountable obstacle of getting the Lenin-Trotsky band of terrorists across the border into Russia. Well, that's where Brother Warburg, chief of the German Secret Police, came in. He loaded all those thugs into sealed freight cars and made all the necessary arrangements for their secret entry into Russia. The rest is history.

The revolution in Russia took place and all members of the royal Romanoff family were murdered.

Now my chief objective is to establish beyond even a remote doubt that communism, so-called, is an integral part of the Illuminati great conspiracy for the enslavement of the entire world. That communism, so-called, is merely their weapon and bogy man word to terrify the peoples of the whole world and that the conquest of Russia and the creation of communism was, in great part, organized by Schiff and the other international bankers right in our own city of New York.

A fantastic story? Yes. Some might even refuse to believe it. Well, for the benefit of any 'doubting Thomas', I will prove it by reminding that just a few years ago Charlie Knickerbocker, a Hearst newspaper columnist, published an interview with John Schiff, grandson of Jacob, in which young Schiff confirmed the entire story and named the figure old Jacob contributed, $20,000,000.

[PART 5]

If anybody still has even a remote doubt that the entire menace of communism was created by the masterminds of the great conspiracy right in our own city of New York, I will cite the following historical fact: All records show that when Lenin and Trotsky engineered the capture of Russia, they operated as heads of the Bolsheviki party. Now, Bolshevism is a purely Russian word.

The masterminds realized that Bolshevism could never be sold as an ideology to any but the Russian people. So in April 1918, Jacob Schiff dispatched Colonel House to Moscow with orders to Lenin, Trotsky, and Stalin, to change the name of their regime to the Communist Party and to adopt the Karl Marx Manifesto as the constitution of the Communist Party. Lenin, Trotsky, and Stalin obeyed, and that year of 1918 was when the Communist party and the menace of communism came into being.

All this is confirmed in Webster's Collegiate Dictionary, Fifth Edition.

In short, communism was created by the capitalists. Thus, until November 11, 1918, the entire fiendish plan of the conspirators worked perfectly. All the great nations, including the United States, were war-weary, devastated, and mourning their dead. Peace was the great universal desire. Thus when it was proposed by Wilson to set up a League of Nations to ensure peace, all the great nations, with no Russian Czar to stand in their way, jumped on that bandwagon without even stopping to read the fine print in that insurance policy.

That is, all but one – the United States – the very one that Schiff and his co-conspirators least expected would balk. And that was their one fatal mistake in that early plot. You see, when Schiff planted Woodrow Wilson in the White House, the conspirators assumed that they had the United States in the proverbial bag. Wilson had been perfectly built up as a great humanitarian. He supposedly became established as a god-man with the American people. There was every reason for the conspirators to have believed that he would easily hornswoggle Congress into buying the League of Nations, 'sight unseen', exactly as the Congress of 1945 bought the United Nations, 'sight unseen'.

But there was one man in the Senate in 1918 who saw through that scheme just as the Russian Czar did in 1814. He was a man of great political stature, almost as great as that of Teddy Roosevelt, and fully as astute. He was highly respected and trusted by all members of both houses of Congress and by the American people. The name of that great and patriotic American was Henry Cabot Lodge, (not the phony of today who called himself *Henry Cabot Lodge, Jr.,* until he was exposed).

Lodge completely unmasked Wilson and kept the United States out of the League of Nations. Here it becomes of great interest to know the real reason for the Wilson League of Nations flop. As I previously stated, Schiff was sent to the United States to carry out four specific assignments:

1. And most important, was to acquire complete control of the US money system.

2. As outlined in the original Weishaupt Illuminati blueprint, he was to find the right kind of men to serve as stooges for the great conspiracy and promote them into the highest offices in our federal government, our Congress, our US Supreme Court, and all federal agencies, such as the State Department, the Pentagon, the Treasury Department, etc.

3. Destroy the unity of the American people by creating minority group strife throughout the nation – especially between the whites and blacks, as outlined in Israel Cohen's book.

4. Create a movement to destroy religion of the United States with Christianity to be the chief target or victim.

In addition, he was strongly reminded of the imperative directive in the Illuminati blueprint to achieve full control of all mass communications media to be used to brainwash the people into believing and accepting all of the maneuverings of the great conspiracy. Schiff was warned that only control of the press, at that time our only mass communications media, would enable him to destroy the unity of the American people.

Now then, Schiff and his co-conspirators did set up the NAACP (the National Association for the Advancement of the Colored People) in 1909 and in 1913 he set up the Anti-Defamation League of the B'nai B'rith. Both were to create the necessary strife, but in the early years, the ADL operated very timidly. Perhaps for fear of a pogrom-like action by an aroused and enraged American people and the NAACP was practically dormant because its white leadership didn't realize that they would have to develop fire-brand Negro leaders, such as Martin 'Lucifer' King for one, to spark the then completely satisfied, contented mass of Negroes.

In addition, he, Schiff, was busy developing and infiltrating the stooges to serve in all high places in our Washington government and in the job of acquiring control of our money system and the creation of the 16th Amendment. He also was very busy with the organizing of the plot for the takeover of Russia. In short, he was kept so busy with all those jobs that he completely overlooked the supreme job of acquiring complete control of our mass communications media. That oversight was a direct cause for Wilson's failure to lure the United States into the League of Nations because when Wilson decided to go to the people to overcome the opposition of the Lodge-controlled Senate, despite his established, but phony reputation as a great humanitarian, he found himself faced by a solidly united people and by a loyal press whose only ideology was Americanism and the American way of life.

At that time, due to the ineptness and ineffectiveness of the ADL and the NAACP, there were no organized minority groups, no Negro problems, no so-called anti-Semitic problems to sway the people's thinking. There were no lefts, there were no rights, no prejudices for crafty exploitations. Thus Wilson's League of Nations appeal fell on deaf ears. That was the end of Woodrow Wilson, the conspirators great humanitarian. He quickly abandoned his crusade and returned to Washington where he shortly died an imbecile brought on by syphilis and that was the end of the League of Nations as a corridor into one-world government.

Of course that debacle was a terrible disappointment to the masterminds of the Illuminati conspiracy, but they were not discouraged. As I have previously stressed, this enemy never quits. They simply decided to reorganize and try from scratch again. By this time Schiff was very old and slow. He knew it. He knew that the conspiracy needed a new younger and more active generalship.

So on his orders, Colonel House and Bernard Barouk organized and set up what they called the Council on Foreign Relations, the new name under which the Illuminati would continue to function in the United States. The hierarchy, officers and directors of the CFR, is composed principally of descendants of the original Illuminati, many of whom who had abandoned their old family name and acquired new Americanized names.

For one example, we have Dillon, who was Secretary of Treasury of the United States, whose original name was Laposky. Another example is Pauley, head of the CBS TV channel, whose true name is Palinsky. The membership of the CFR is approximately 1,000 in number and contains the heads of virtually every industrial empire in America such as Blough, president of the US Steel Corporation, Rockefeller, king of the oil industry, Henry Ford, II, and so on. And of course, all the international bankers. Also, the heads of the tax-free foundations are officers and/or active CFR members. In short, all the men who provide the money and the influence to elect the CFR-chosen Presidents of the United States, the Congressmen, the Senators, and who decide the appointments of our various Secretaries of State, of the Treasury, of every important federal agency, are members of the CFR and they are very obedient members indeed.

Now just to cement that fact, I will mention the names of the United States Presidents who were members of the CFR: Franklin Roosevelt, Herbert Hoover, Dwight D. Eisenhower, Jack Kennedy. Others who were considered for the presidency are Thomas E. Dewey, Adlai Stevenson, Nixon, and vice-president of a CFR subsidiary, Barry Goldwater. Among the important cabinet members of the various administrations we have John Foster Dulles, Allen Dulles, Cordell Hull, John J. McCloy, Robert Morganthau, Clarence Dillon, Rusk, McNamara, and just to emphasize the red color of the CFR we have as members such men as Alger Hiss, Ralph Bunche, Pasvolsky, Harry Dexter White (real name Weiss), Owen Lattimore, Phillip Jaffey, etc. etc. Simultaneously, they were flooding thousands of homosexuals and other blackmailable characters into all the federal agencies from the White House down. Remember Johnson's great friends, Jenkins and Bobby Baker?

Now there were many jobs the new CFR had to accomplish. They required much help. So their first job was to set up various subsidiaries to whom they assigned special objectives. I can't name all the subsidiaries in this recording, but the following are a few: the Foreign Policy Association (FPA), the World Affairs Council (WAC), the Business Advisory Council (BAC), the notorious ADA (Americans for Democratic Action virtually headed by Walter Ruther), the notorious '13-13' in Chicago, Barry Goldwater was, and no doubt still is, a vice-president of one of the CFR subsidiaries. In addition, the CFR set up special committees in every state in the Union to whom they assigned the various local state operations.

Simultaneously, the Rothschilds set up similar CFR-like control groups in England, France,

Germany, and other Nations, to control world conditions and cooperate with the CFR to bring about another world war. But the CFR's first and foremost job was to get complete control of our mass communications media.

The control of the press was assigned to Rockefeller. Thus, Henry Luce, who recently died, was financed to set up a number of national magazines, among them *Life*, *Time*, *Fortune*, and others, which publish *"USSR in America"*. The Rockefellers also directly or indirectly financed the Cowles Brothers' *"Look"* magazine and a chain of newspapers. They also financed a man named Sam Newhouse to buy up and build a chain of newspapers all over the country. And the late Eugene Myer, one of the founders of CFR, bought the *Washington Post*, *Newsweek*, the *Weekly Magazine*, and other publications.

At the same time, the CFR began to develop and nurture a new breed of scurrilous columnists and editorials writers such as Walter Lippman, Drew Pearson, the Alsops, Herbert Matthews, Erwin Canham, and others of that ilk who called themselves Liberals who proclaimed that Americanism is isolationism, that isolationism is war mongerism, that anti-communism, is anti-Semitism and racism.

All that took time of course, but today, our entire press, except for some local small town papers and weeklies, published by patriotic organizations, is completely controlled by CFR stooges and thus they finally succeeded in breaking us up into a nation of quarreling, wrangling, squabbling, hating factions. Now if you still wonder about this slanted news and outright lies you read in your paper, you now have the answer. To the Lehmans, Goldman-Sachs, Kuhn-Loebs, and the Warburgs, the CFR assigned the job of getting control of the motion picture industry (Hollywood), radio, and television, and believe you me, they succeeded.

If you still wonder about the strange propaganda broadcast by the Ed Morrows, Jeff Huntley, Howard K. Smith, Erick Severide, Drew Pearson and others of that ilk, you now have the answer. If you wonder about all the smut, sex, pornography, and mixed marriage films you see in your movie theater and on your TV set, all of which is demoralizing our youth, you have the answer.

The whole story of the CFR conspiracy take-over of our mass communications media is far to long to included in this recording but you can find it in the news bulletin #125 entitled *"How to Get the 'Reds' Out of Communications Media".* It was published and brought up to date by the Cinema Educational Guild. It tells in detail how the press, movies, the TV and Radio have been, and still are, used to brainwash the people and demoralize our youth and they have been and still are encouraging and creating sympathy for the rioting Negroes civil rights lawlessness. You can get a copy of this news bulletin by writing to the Cinema Educational Guild, PO Box 46205, Hollywood California.

Now to refresh your memory, let's go back for a moment. Wilson's flop had torpedoed all chances of transforming that League of Nations into the conspirators' hoped-for one-world government housing. So the Jacob Schiff plot had to be done all over again, and they organized the CFR to do it. We also know how successfully the CFR did that job of brainwashing and destroying the unity of the American people.

But, as was the case with the Schiff plot, the climax and the creation of a new housing for their one world government required another world war. A war that would be even more horrible and more devastating than the first world war in order to get the people of the world to again clamor for peace and a means to end all wars. But the CFR realized that the aftermath of World War II would have to be more carefully planned so that there would be no escape from the new one-world trap, another League of Nations, that would emerge from the new war; the trap we now know as the United Nations. And they hit upon a perfect strategy to ensure that no-one escaped. Here is how they did it.

In 1943, in the midst of the war, they prepared the framework for the United Nations and it was handed over to Roosevelt and our State Department to be given birth by Alger Hiss, Pasvolsky, Dalton Trumbull, and other American traitors, thus making the whole scheme a United States baby. Then to fix our parenthood, New York City was to become the nursery for the monstrosity. After that we could hardly walk out on our own baby now could we? Anyway, that's how the conspirators figured it would work, and so far it has. And the liberal Rockefeller donated the land for the United Nations building.

The United Nations' charter was written by Alger Hiss, Pasvolsky, Dalton Trumbull, and other CFR stooges. A phony, so-called, UN conference was set up in San Francisco in 1945. All the, so-called, representatives of 50-odd nations gathered there and promptly signed the Charter and the despicable traitor, Alger Hiss, flew to Washington with it, elatedly submitted it to our Senate, and the Senate (elected by our people to safeguard our security) signed the Charter without so much as reading it. The question is, how many of our Senators were even then traitorous stooges of the CFR? Anyway, it was thus that the people accepted the United Nations as a holy of holies, and enabled traitor Earl Warren to virtually destroy our constitution by basing all his traitorous decisions on the UN Charter, thus making that Charter virtually our law of the land.

However, for all the dirty work that had to be done to solidify the UN, the new housing of the one–world plot, they still required the aid of our leaders in Washington. So now I will emphasize the fiendish cleverness of the CFR masterminds. To the vast majority of the American people, our foreign policy for many years has been a complete enigma. Most of us simply can't understand why this great nation is seemingly floundering so helplessly in the art of diplomacy. We can't understand why our leaders are seemingly so confused and bewildered in all their dealings with Moscow, France, and other nations and with the UN. We always hear them proclaiming that in view of our overwhelming economic and military superiority we must always lead from strength. Yet, at all the summit meetings and conferences they cringe and stammer, and stutter, and so to speak come out with their tails between their hind legs. We can't understand the foreign aid to Tito an avowed enemy, to Poland an avowed enemy, to all the avowed Communists nations. We can't understand why the expenditure of hundreds of billions of dollars has failed to slow down, let alone stop, the march of commUNism. We are perplexed by the seeming ineptness of the State Department, the defense department, the CIA, the USIA, of all our federal agencies.

Again and again and again we have been startled, shocked, bewildered, and horrified by their mistakes in Berlin, in Korea, in Laos, in Katanga, in Cuba, in Vietnam – mistakes that always favored the enemy, never the United States. Under the law of averages, they should have made at least one or two mistakes in our favor, but they never did.

What's the answer? The answer is the CFR and the parts played by their subsidiaries and stooges in

Washington. Thus we know that complete control of our foreign relation policy is the key to the success of the entire Illuminati one-world order plot. Here is the further proof:

Earlier I fully established that Schiff and his gang had financed the Lenin-Trotsky-Stalin takeover of Russia and fashioned its communist regime into becoming their chief instrument to keep the world in turmoil and to finally terrorize all of us into seeking peace in a UN one-world government. But the conspirators knew that the Moscow gang could not become such an instrument until, and unless, the whole world would accept the communist regime as the legitimate 'de jure' government of Russia.

Only one thing could accomplish that – recognition by the United States. The conspirators figured that the whole world would follow our lead and that's and that's when the Wilson flop very nearly wrecked the entire plot. Throughout the following three Republican administrations the CFR pulled every trick in their bag to induce Harding, Coolidge, and Hoover, to grant that recognition. But all three refused. As a result, in the late 1920's, the Stalin regime was in dire straits. Despite all purges and secret police controls, the Russian people were growing more and more resistive. It is a matter of record, admitted by Lipdenoff, that during 1931 and 1932, Stalin and his whole gang were always packed and ready for instant flight.

Then in November 1932, the conspirators achieved their greatest coup. They landed Franklin Roosevelt in the White House, crafty, unscrupulous, and utterly without conscience, that charlatan traitor turned the trick for them. Without even asking consent of Congress, he unlawfully proclaimed recognition for the Stalin regime. That did it. And exactly as the conspirators figured, the whole world did follow our lead. Automatically that squelched the previously growing resistance movement of the Russian people. That automatically launched the greatest menace the civilized world has ever known. The rest is too well known to need repeating.

We know how Roosevelt and his traitorous State Department kept building up the communist menace right here in our country and thus throughout the world. We know how he perpetuated that Pearl Harbor atrocity for his excuse to hurl us into World War II. We know all about his secret meetings with Stalin at Yalta. And how he, with Eisenhower's help, delivered the Balkans and Berlin to Moscow. And last, but by no means least, we know that that 20th century 'Benedict Arnold' not only dragged us into that new corridor, the United Nations, into the one-world government, but he actually schemed all the arrangements to plant it within our country. In short, the day that Roosevelt entered the White House, the CFR conspirators regained full control of our foreign relations machinery and firmly established the United Nations as the housing for the Illuminati one-world government.

I wish to stress one other very vital point. That Wilson's League of Nations flop brought Schiff and his gang to the realization that control of *just* the Democratic Party was not enough. True, they could create a crisis during the Republican administration as they did in 1929 with their Federal Reserve manufactured crash and depression which would bring another Democrat stooge back into the White House, but they realized that a four-year disruption in their control of our foreign relation policies could play havoc with the progress of their conspiracy. It could even break up their entire strategy as it almost did before Roosevelt saved it with his recognition of the Stalin regime.

Thereupon, after that Wilson debacle, they began to formulate plans to achieve control of *both* of our national parties. But that posed a problem for them. Manpower. Stooges in the Republican Party.

Also added manpower for the Democratic Party, because control of just the man in the White House would not be enough. They would have to provide that man with trained stooges for his entire cabinet, men to head the State Department, the Treasury Department, the Pentagon, the CFR, the USIA, etc.

In short, every member of the various cabinets would have to be a chosen tool of the CFR, such as Rusk and McNamara, also all the undersecretaries and assistant secretaries. That would give the conspirators absolute control of all our policies, both domestic and most important, foreign. That course of action would require a reserve pool of trained stooges, instantaneously ready for administrative changes and for all other exigencies.

All such stooges would of necessity have to be men of national reputation, high in the esteem of the people, but they would have to be men without honor, without scruple, without conscience – men who would be vulnerable to blackmail. It is needless for me to stress how well the CFR succeeded. The immortal Joe McCarthy fully revealed that there are thousands of such security risks in all federal agencies.

Scott MacLeod unmasked thousands more, and you know the price Ortepta has had to pay, and is still paying, for his expositions before a Senate Committee of the traitors in the State Department. And you know that the men in the State Department, who delivered Cuba to Castro, have not only been shielded, but promoted.

[PART 6]

Now let's go back to the crux of the whole one-world government plot and the maneuvering necessary to create another League of Nations to house such a government.

As I have already stated, the conspirators knew that only another world war was vital for the success of their plot. It would have to be such a horrifying world war that the peoples of the world would cry out for the creation of some kind of a world organization that could assure everlasting peace. But how could such a war be brought about? All the European nations were at peace. None had any quarrels with their neighboring nations, and certainly their stooges in Moscow wouldn't dare to start a war. Even Stalin realized that it would mean the overthrow of his regime unless, so-called patriotism would weld the Russian people behind him.

But the conspirators had to have a war. They had to find or create some kind of an incident to launch it. And they found it, in a little inconspicuous and repulsive little man who called himself Adolf Hitler.

Hitler, an impecunious Austrian house painter, had been a corporal in the German army. He made the defeat of Germany into a personal grievance. He began to rabble rouse about it in the Munich, Germany area. He began to spout about restoring the greatness of the German Empire and the might of the German soldiery. He advocated the restoration of the old German military to be used to conquer the whole world. Strangely enough, Hitler, the little clown that he was, could deliver a rabble rousing speech and he did have a certain kind of magnetism. But the new authorities in Germany didn't want anymore wars and they promptly threw the obnoxious Austrian house painter into a prison cell.

Aha! Here was the man, decided the conspirators, who, properly directed and financed, could be the key to another world war. So while he was in prison, they had Rudolph Hess and Goering write a book which they titled *Mein Kompf* and attributed the authorship to Hitler, exactly as Lipdenoff wrote *Mission to Moscow* and attributed the authorship to Joseph Davies, then our ambassador to Russia and a stooge of the CFR. In *Mein Kompf,* Hitler, the pseudo-author, outlined his grievances and how he would restore the German people to their former greatness.

The conspirators then arrange for a wide circulation of the book among the German people in order to arouse a fanatical following for him. On his release from prison (also arranged by the conspirators), they began to groom him and finance him to travel to other parts of Germany to deliver his rabble rousing speeches. Soon he gathered a growing following among other veterans of the war and that soon spread to the masses who began to see in him a saviour for their beloved Germany.

Then came his leadership of what he called his *'brown shirt army'* and the march on Berlin. That required a great deal of financing, but the Rothschilds, the Warburgs, and others of the conspirators provided all the money he needed. Gradually Hitler became the idol of the German people and then they overthrew the Von Hindenburg government and Hitler became the new Fuhrer. But that still was no reason for a war.

The rest of the world watched Hitler's rise, but saw no reason to interfere in what was distinctly a domestic condition within Germany. Certainly none of the other Nations felt it was a reason for another war against Germany and the German people were not yet incited into enough of a frenzy to commit any acts against any neighboring nation, not even against France, that would lead to a war. The conspirators realized they would have to create such a frenzy – a frenzy that would cause the German people to throw caution to the winds and at the same time, horrify the whole world. And incidentally, *Mein Kompf* was actually a follow-up of Karl Marx's book *A World Without Jews.*

The conspirators suddenly remembered how

the Schiff-Rothschild gang had engineered the pogroms in Russia which slaughtered many, many thousands of Jews and created a world-wide hatred for Russia and they decided to use that same unconscionable trick to inflame the new Hitler-led German people into a murderous hatred of the Jews.

Now it is true that the German people never had any particular affection for the Jews, but neither did they have an ingrained hatred for them. Such a hatred would have to be manufactured, so Hitler was to create it. This idea more than appealed to Hitler. He saw in it the grisly gimmick to make him the God-man of the German people.

Thus craftily inspired and coached by his financial advisers, the Warburgs, Rothschilds, and all the Illuminati masterminds, he blamed the Jews for the hated Versailles Treaty and for the financial ruination that followed the war. The rest is history. We know all about the Hitler concentration camps and the incineration of hundreds of thousands of Jews. Not the 6,000,000 nor even the 600,000 claimed by the conspirators, but it was enough.

And here let me reiterate how little the internationalist bankers, the Rothschilds, Schiffs, Lehmans, Warburgs, Barouks, care about their racial brethren who were the victims of their nefarious schemes. In their eyes, the slaughter of the several hundred thousand innocent Jews by Hitler didn't bother them at all. They considered it a necessary sacrifice to further their Illuminati one-world plot just as the slaughter of the many millions in the wars that followed, was a similar necessary sacrifice. And here is another grisly detail about those concentration camps. Many of the Hitler soldier executioners in those camps had previously been sent to Russia to acquire their arts of torture and brutalization, so as to emphasize the horrors of the atrocities.

All this created a new world-wide hatred for the German people, but it still did not provide a cause for a war. Thereupon Hitler was incited to demand the Sudetenland. You remember how Chamberlain, and the then diplomats of Czechoslovakia and France, surrendered to that demand. That led to further Hitlerian demands for territories in Poland and in the French Saar territories.

Those demands were rejected.

Then came his pact with Stalin. Hitler had been screaming hatred against communism. Oh how he ranted against communism! But actually nazism was nothing but socialism, and communism is, in fact, socialism. But Hitler disregarded all that. He entered into a pact with Stalin to attack and divide Poland between them. While Stalin marched into one part of Poland (for which he was never blamed – the Illuminati masterminds saw to that), Hitler launched a blitzkrieg on Poland from his side. The conspirators finally had their new world war. And what a horrible war it was!

And in 1945, the conspirators finally achieved the United Nations, their new housing for their one–world government. And truly amazing, all of the American people hailed this foul outfit as a holy of holies. Even after all the true facts about how the UN was created were revealed, the American people continued to worship that evil outfit. Even after Alger Hiss was unmasked as a Soviet spy and traitor, the American people continued to believe in the UN.

Even after I had publicly revealed the secret agreement between Hiss and Molotov, that a Russian would *always* be the head of military secretariat and by that token, the real master of the UN, most of the American people continued to believe that the UN could do no wrong. Even after Trig D. Lee, the first Secretary general of the UN confirmed that Hiss-Molotov secret agreement in his book *"For the Cause of Peace",* the vast majority of our people refused to loose faith in the UN.

Even after the truth about the Korean war was revealed, how the Russian General Varsilius, head of that UN military secretariat was given a leave of absence by the UN so that he could take command of the North Koreans and Red Chinese who were fighting the so-called UN police action under our own General McArthur, who, by order of the UN, was fired by the pusillanimous Truman in order to prevent his winning that war, our people still believed in the UN despite our 150,000 sons who were murdered and maimed in that war, the people continued to regard the UN as a sure means for peace.

Even after it was revealed in 1951 that the UN, using our own American soldiers under UN command, under UN flag, in collusion with our traitorous State Department and the Pentagon had been invading many small cities in California and Texas in order to perfect their plan for the complete takeover of our country, most of our people brushed it off and continued their belief that the UN is a holy of holies.

Do you know that the UN Charter was written by traitor Alger Hiss, Molotov, and Vyshinsky? That Hiss and Molotov had made that secret agreement that the military chief of the UN was always to be a Russian appointed by Moscow? Do you know that at their secret meetings at Yalta, Roosevelt and Stalin, at the behest of the Illuminati operating as the CFR, decided that the UN must be placed on American soil?

Do you know that most of the UN Charter was copied intact, word for word, from the Marx Manifesto and the Russian, so-called constitution? Do you know that the only two Senators who voted against the UN so-called treaty, were the only two Senators who had read it? Do you know that since the UN was founded, communist enslavement has grown from 250,000,000 to 1,000,000,000?

Do you know that since the UN was founded to

insure peace, there have been at least 20 major wars incited by the UN, just as they are now inciting a war against Middle Rhodesia? Do you know that under the UN set up, the American taxpayers have been forced to make up the UN Treasury deficit of many millions of dollars because of Russia's refusal to pay her share? Do you know that the UN has never passed a resolution condemning Russia or her so-called satellites, but always condemns our Allies?

Do you know that J. Edgar Hoover said the overwhelming majority of the communist delegations to the UN are espionage agents and now 66 Senators voted for a Consular Treaty to open our entire country to Russian spies and saboteurs? Do you know that the UN helps Russia's conquest of the world by preventing the free world from taking any action whatsoever except to debate each new aggression in the UN General Assembly?

Do you know that at the time of the Korean War there were 60 Nations in the UN, yet 95% of the UN forces were our American sons and practically 100% of the cost was paid by the United States taxpayers?

And surely you know that the UN policy during the Korean and Vietnam Wars was to prevent us from winning that wars? Do you know that all the battle plans of General McArthur had to go first to the UN to be relayed to Varsilius, Commander of the North Koreans and Red Chinese, and that any future wars fought by our sons under the UN flag would have to be fought under the control of the UN Security Council?

Do you know that the UN has never done anything about the 80,000 Russian Mongolian troops that occupy Hungary?

Where was the UN when the Hungarian freedom fighters were slaughtered by the Russians? Do you know that the UN and its peace army turned the Congo over to the communists? Do you know that the UN's own so-called peace force was used to crush, rape, and kill the white anti-communists in Katanga?

Do you know that the UN stood by and did nothing while Red China invaded Laos and Vietnam? That it did nothing while Nehru invaded Goe and other Portuguese territories? Do you know that the UN was directly responsible for aiding Castro? That it does absolutely nothing about the many thousands of Cuban youngsters who are shipped to Russia for communist indoctrination.

Do you know that Adlai Stevenson, of all people, said the free world must expect to lose more and more decisions in the UN. Do you know that the UN openly proclaims that its chief objective is a one-world government which means one-world laws, one-world court, one-world army, one-world navy, one-world air-force, one-world schools, and a one-world church in which Christianity would be prohibited?

Do you know that a UN law has been passed to disarm all American citizens and to transfer all our armed forces to the UN? Such a law was secretly signed by 'saint' Jack Kennedy in 1961. Do you realize how that fits in with Article 47, paragraph 3, of the UN Charter, which states, I quote: *"the military staff committee of the UN shall be responsible through the Security Council for the strategic direction of all armed forces placed at the disposal of the Security Council."* And when and if all our armed forces are transferred to the UN, your sons would be forced to serve and die under UN command all over the world. This will happen unless you fight to get the US out of the UN.

Do you know that Congressmen James B. Utt has submitted a bill to get the US out of the UN and a resolution to prevent our President from forcing us to support the UN embargoes on Rhodesia? Well, he has. And many people all over the country are writing to their representatives to support the Utt bill and resolution. And did you know that to off-set the Utt bill and resolution, fifty Congressmen, spear-headed by Schweiker and Moorhead of Pennsylvania, have introduced a bill to immediately transfer all our armed forces to the UN? Can you imagine such brazen treason? Is your Congressman one of those fifty traitors? Find out and take immediate action against him and help Congressman Utt.

Now do you know that the National Council of Churches passed a resolution in San Francisco which states that the United States will soon have to subordinate its will to that of the UN and that all American citizens must be prepared to accept it? Is your church a member of the National Council of Churches? In connection with that, bear in mind that God is never mentioned in the UN Charter and their meetings are never opened with prayer. The creators of the UN stipulated in advance that there should be no mention of God or Jesus Christ in the UN Charter or in its UN headquarters. Does your pastor subscribe to that? Find out!

Furthermore, do you know that the great majority of the so-called nations in the UN are anti-christianity, that the UN is a completely godless organization by orders of its creators, the CFR Illuminati. Have you heard enough of the truth the Illuminati's United Nations? Do you want to leave your sons and our precious country to the unholy mercy of the Illuminati's United Nations?

If you don't, write, telegraph, or phone your Representatives and Senators that they must support Congressman Utt's bill to get the US out of the UN and the UN out of the US. Do it today, now, before you forget! It is the only salvation for your sons and for our country.

[4. Destroy religion.]

Now I have one more vital message to deliver. As I told you, one of the four specific assignments Rothschild gave Jacob Schiff was to create a movement to destroy religion in the United States with Christianity to be the chief target. For a very obvious reason, the Anti-Defamation League wouldn't dare to attempt it because such an attempt could create the most terrible blood bath in the history of the world, not only for the ADL and the conspirators, but for the millions of innocent Jews.

Schiff turned that job over to Rockefeller for another specific reason. The destruction of Christianity could be accomplished only by those who are entrusted to preserve it. By the pastors – the men of the cloth.

As a starter, John D. Rockefeller picked up a young, so-called, Christian minister by the name of Dr. Harry F. Ward – Reverend Ward if you please. At that time he was teaching religion at the Union Theological Seminary. Rockefeller found a very willing 'Judas' in this Reverend and thereupon in 1907, he financed him to set up the *Methodist Foundation of Social Service* and Ward's job was to teach bright young men to become, so-called ministers of Christ and to place them as pastors of churches.

While teaching them to become ministers, the

Reverend Ward also taught them how to subtly and craftily preach to their congregations that the entire story of Christ was a myth to cast doubts on the divinity of Christ, to cast doubts about the virgin Mary – in short, to cast doubts on Christianity as a whole. It was not to be a direct attack, but much of it to be done by crafty insinuation that was to be applied, in particular, to the youth in the Sunday schools.

Remember Lenin's statement, *"Give me just one generation of youth and I'll transform the whole world."* Then in 1908, the Methodist Foundation of Social Service, which incidentally was America's first communist front organization, changed its name to *the Federal Council of Churches*. By 1950, the Federal Council of Churches was becoming very suspect so in 1950 they changed the name to the *National* Council of Churches.

Do I have to tell you more about how this National Council of Churches is deliberately destroying faith in Christianity? I don't think so. But this I will tell you. If you are a member of any congregation whose pastor and church are members of this Judas organization, you – your contributions – are helping the Illuminati's plot to destroy Christianity and your faith in God and Jesus Christ thus you are deliberately delivering your children to be indoctrinated with disbelief in God and Church and which can easily transform them into atheists.

Find out immediately if your Church is a member of the National Council of Churches and, for the love of God and your children, if it is, withdraw from it at once. However, let me warn you that the same destroy-religion process has been infiltrated into other denominations. If you have seen the Negro march on Selma and other such demonstrations, you have seen how the Negro mobs are led and encouraged by ministers, and even Catholic priests and nuns, who march along with them. As a matter of fact, the Mormon Church is about the only one I know of that is clean of that kind of Judas infiltration.

Of course there are many individual churches and pastors who are honest and sincere. Find one such for yourself and for your children. Incidentally, this same Reverend Harry F. Ward was also one of the founders of the American Civil Liberties Union, a notorious pro-communist organization. He was the actual head of it from 1920 to 1940. He also was a co-founder of the American League Against War and Fascism which, under Browder, became the Communist Party of the United States.

In short, Ward's entire background reeked of communism and he was identified as a member of the communist party. He died a vicious traitor to both his church and country. And this was the man old John D. Rockefeller picked and financed to destroy America's Christian religion in accordance with the orders given to Schiff by the Rothschilds.

In conclusion I have this to say: You probably are familiar with the story of how one Dr. Frankenstein created a monster to do his will of destroying his chosen victims but how instead in the end, that monster turned on his own creator, Frankenstein, and destroyed him. Well, the Illuminati CFR has created a monster called the United Nations, who is supported by their minority groups, rioting negroes, the traitorous mass communications media, and the traitors in Washington was created to destroy the American people.

We know all about that many-headed hydra-monster and we know the names of those who created that monster. We know all their names and I predict that one fine day the American people will come fully awake and cause that very monster to destroy its creator. True! The majority of our people are still being brainwashed, deceived, and deluded by our traitorous press, TV, and radio, and by our traitors in Washington, but surely by now enough is known about the UN to stamp out that outfit as a deadly poisonous rattlesnake in our midst.

My only wonder, is what it will take to awaken and arouse our people to the full proof? Perhaps this record will do it. A hundred thousand or a million copies of this record can do it. I pray to God it will. And I pray to Him to inspire you, all of you, to spread this story via this record, to all loyal Americans in your community.

You can do it by playing it to study groups assembled in your homes, at meetings of the American Legion, the VFW, the DAR, all other civic groups and women's clubs – especially the women's clubs who have their sons lives at stake. With this record, I have provided you with the weapon that will destroy the monster. For the love of God, of our Country, and of your children, use it! Get a copy of it into every American home.

———

Myron Fagan,
Illuminati CFR Recording, 1967

———

[Originally distributed as a 3-LP record set. Later, audio cassettes became available – now freely available in mp3 format on the internet.]

[This transcript is a composite from several posted on the internet, checked and reconciled to be as authentic as possible with the six-part audio.]

Other titles

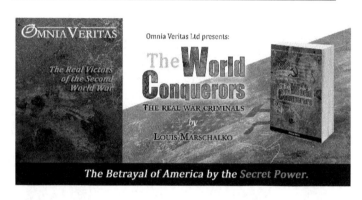

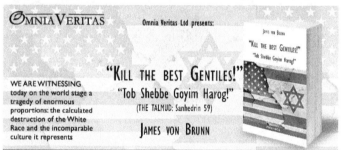

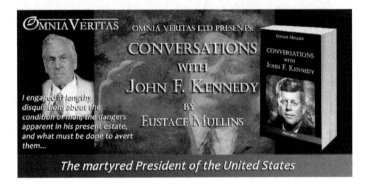

Omnia Veritas Ltd presents:

MURDER BY INJECTION

by

EUSTACE MULLINS

THE STORY OF THE MEDICAL CONSPIRACY AGAINST AMERICA

The cynicism and malice of these conspirators is something beyond the imagination of most Americans.

OMNIA VERITAS LTD PRESENTS:

MY LIFE IN CHRIST

BY

EUSTACE MULLINS

Christ did not wish to be followed by robots and sleepwalkers, He desired man to awaken, and to attain the full use of his earthly powers.

THIS is the story of my life in Christ

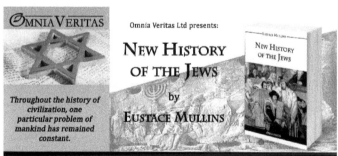

Omnia Veritas Ltd presents:

NEW HISTORY OF THE JEWS

by

EUSTACE MULLINS

Throughout the history of civilization, one particular problem of mankind has remained constant.

Only one people has irritated its host nations in every part of the civilized world

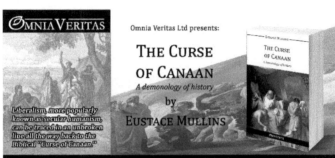

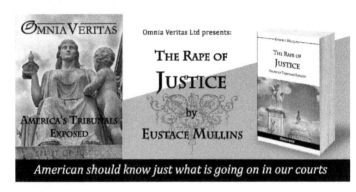

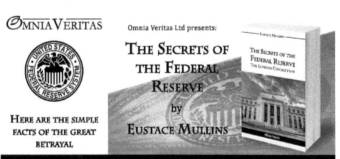

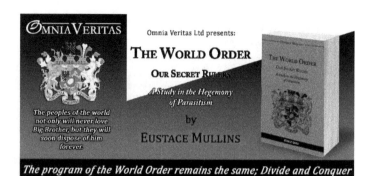

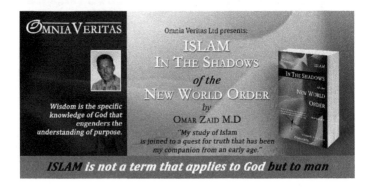

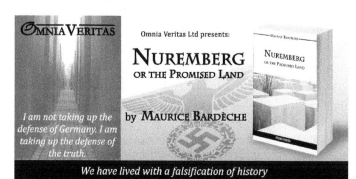

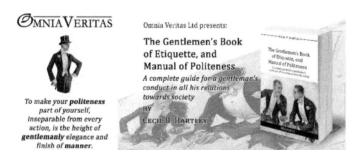

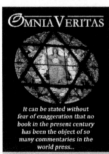

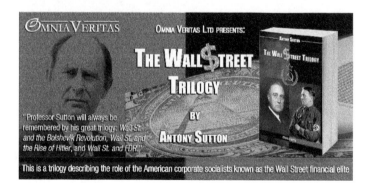

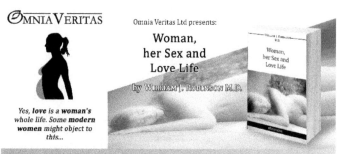

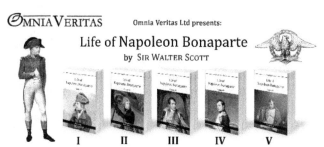

Lightning Source UK Ltd.
Milton Keynes UK
UKHW010958080223
416610UK00015B/1666